THE LITTLE BOOK OF

BIG
Aussie
ICONS

CRAIG SCUTT

The Big Nobe

g Crab

The Big Str...

The Big B...

The Big B

The Big Orange

The Big Worm

The Five Mile Press

THE BIG
BANANA
COFFS HARBOUR

Celebrating 40 Years

The Five Mile Press Pty Ltd
1 Centre Road, Scoresby
Victoria 3179 Australia
www.fivemile.com.au

First published 2009

Printed in China 5 4 3 2

Compiled and edited by Rachel Williams
Design by Kristy Lund
Images sourced from Wikimedia Commons, Newspix and AAP.

THE LITTLE BOOK OF

BIG

Aussie

ICONS

The Big Merino

The Big Bull

The Big Staircase

The Big Dinosaur

Big Chook

The Big

The R:

The Big Stockwhip

The Big Pineapple

The Big Gumboot

The Big Captain Cook

The Big Cassowary

g Scotsma'

The Big Crocodile

The Big Stubby

Acknowledgements

The Editor would like to thank the following people for a number of big reasons:

Yvette Sittrop and Maja Vatric, for their extra large image research.
The many Big Things super-sleuths such as Trish from the
Muswellbrook Visitor's Centre, who gave us all the vital info
we were after. And of course, a big congratulations to
The Big Croc of Wyndham, Australia, who had its 21st birthday
while this book was being compiled.

About the author

Craig Scutt is an author and freelance writer. Long ago, a visit to Swan Hill,
home of the Big Murray Cod, gave him his first big experience. He was totally blown
away by the colossal cod's outstanding unnatural beauty, not to mention the hot
tourist posing beside it. What he loves most about Big Things is that each one
represents a bunch of visionaries crazy enough to make them in the first place.
Craig hopes that *The Little Book of Big Aussie Icons* will encourage more people
to get out there and show the Big Things the big love they deserve.

Contents

BIG is Beautiful.

Making things big is part of being in the Land Down Under.

Australia's landmass is 7,692,030 square kilometres. That is the same as thirty two Great Britains laid out side by side, neatly, in a row. To fill up a country that size, you're going to need a few Big Things.

Stick a super-sized Scotsman on the side of a motel, or a colossal Crab on a restaurant rooftop, and voilà, you're on the tourist map.

In 1964, the Big Banana started an avalanche of models that today make up Australia's kitsch cultural heritage in the form of Big Aussie icons.

It was an enormous leap of faith taken by John Landy (the owner), Alan Chapman (the engineer), Alan Harvey (the builder) and the local banana growers' federation (the money) to produce the Big Banana, but it sure has worked.

The aim was to attract motorists to buy Landy's bananas from his roadside stall. But the Big Banana did much more than that. It attracted our imaginations, aroused our childish curiosity, and most importantly, it made us laugh out loud.

As we speedily approach the 50th anniversary of the Big Banana, there are now more than 150 Big Things scattered across the country.

Some outdo others, but they all get to be called Big Things as long as they're substantially bigger than the thing they represent. At times, such a definition seems a bit unfair, as in the case of massive models like the Big Uluru and the Big Whale Shark, neither of which have much chance of being as large as the real thing.

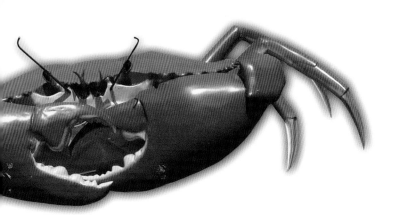

In the original Greek sense of the word, every Big Thing is an icon: a likeness or representation of something. They are also icons if we use the word's modern meaning, as they symbolise something greater than what they merely represent.

The Big Poo was dropped in protest, the Big Dugong is a symbol for endangered wildlife and conservation, and the Big Pineapple is a material and cultural reference point for millions of people who have posed beside it.

As a collective, Big Things light up the landscape, stir the senses, and fire the emotions of everyone who lives and travels throughout this great big nation. They dare you to explore parts of the country you'd otherwise ignore. They challenge you to explain why anyone would go to such an effort to build them. They make long forays into the bush seem abundantly worthwhile. And once you've experienced the rush that is your first Big Thing, there is a very good chance you'll go searching for more.

In compiling this collection of Australia's funniest and most iconic Big Things, we have inevitably had to cull many favourites. Any list is subjective and shortening ours caused heartache and pain to many here at The Five Mile Press.

We want to make it abundantly clear, in writing, that just because a Big Thing isn't in this book does not mean that it is not iconic.

We rated the Big Things based on what we felt they symbolised, how they looked, and how they made us feel. It doesn't get much more subjective than that.

Of course we would have liked to include entries that ended up getting the chop, but in what are supposedly Ned Kelly's last words, 'Such is life'. And, as Australia's biggest icon of all who has had three Big Things built in his honour, he should know.

Icons come in all shapes and sizes, but it's always the big ones we remember.

BIG Aussie ICONS

The Big Boxing Croc, Humpty Doo

The Big Stockwhip, Acacia

The Big Crocodile, Wyndham

The Big Staircase, Perth

The Big Ram, Wagin

The Big Kangaroo, Border Village

The Big Mandarin

Big Miner

The Big Stockwhip

Guitar

The Big Galah

The Big Boxing Croc

STOCKMANS CORNER

The Big Bull

The Big Captain Cook

The Big Trooper

The Big Mango

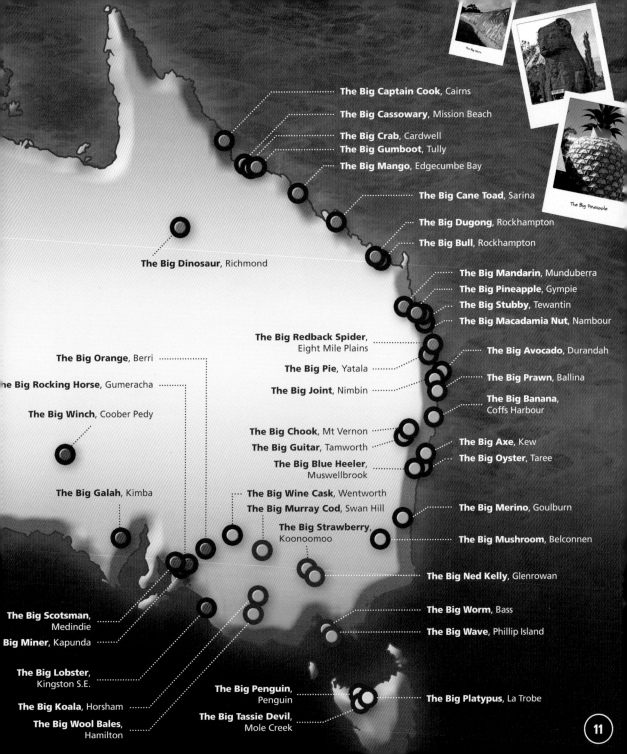

The Big Captain Cook, Cairns

The Big Cassowary, Mission Beach

The Big Crab, Cardwell
The Big Gumboot, Tully
The Big Mango, Edgecumbe Bay

The Big Cane Toad, Sarina

The Big Dugong, Rockhampton

The Big Bull, Rockhampton

The Big Dinosaur, Richmond

The Big Mandarin, Munduberra
The Big Pineapple, Gympie
The Big Stubby, Tewantin
The Big Macadamia Nut, Nambour

The Big Redback Spider, Eight Mile Plains

The Big Avocado, Durandah

The Big Orange, Berri

The Big Pie, Yatala

The Big Prawn, Ballina

he Big Rocking Horse, Gumeracha

The Big Joint, Nimbin

The Big Banana, Coffs Harbour

The Big Winch, Coober Pedy

The Big Chook, Mt Vernon
The Big Guitar, Tamworth

The Big Axe, Kew
The Big Oyster, Taree

The Big Blue Heeler, Muswellbrook

The Big Galah, Kimba

The Big Wine Cask, Wentworth
The Big Murray Cod, Swan Hill

The Big Merino, Goulburn

The Big Strawberry, Koonoomoo

The Big Mushroom, Belconnen

The Big Ned Kelly, Glenrowan

The Big Scotsman, Medindie

Big Miner, Kapunda

The Big Worm, Bass

The Big Wave, Phillip Island

The Big Lobster, Kingston S.E.

The Big Penguin, Penguin

The Big Platypus, La Trobe

The Big Koala, Horsham

The Big Wool Bales, Hamilton

The Big Tassie Devil, Mole Creek

The Big Horn

The Big Pineapple

(11)

The Big Captain Cook

The Big Dugong

The Big Dinosaur

arin

e Big

The Big Cassowary

Resort

OSAURUS KO

The Big Cane Toad

The Big Bull

The Big Gumboot

Queensland

The Big Macadamia Nut

Where it's at:

Rockhampton, 638 km north of Brisbane and just north of the Tropic of Capricorn.

Vitals:

DOB: Date of calving unknown but records show they miraculously appeared sometime before 1983.

Introducing...

The BIG Bulls

Now here are some Big Things to go really nuts about. The Big Bulls are the champion cattle creations in a city that's jam-packed with bovine beauties. Break out your Wranglers, munch on a steak, it's time to moo-ve around and check out the Beef Capital of Australia.

Rumour has it:

A lucky Rockhampton council worker has the choice job of replacing the bulls' testicles. Apparently they disappear from the city sculptures on a regular basis but nobody's ever admitted to taking them.

Did you know?

Pop culture travel website, Jaunted.com, rated Rockhampton as a top 'mancation' destination as it is 'full of testosterone and bucking bronco rides.'

Starring role:

Reports of thieves making off with the Big Bulls' naughty bits have been popping up in local and national press for decades. It's probably only a matter of time before someone makes a movie on the mystery.

Anything else I should know?

Age journalist Anneli Knight has encouraged locals to revel in Rockhampton's self-proclaimed status as Australia's 'Beef Capital' because they feel angry that the city wasn't made the capital of a seventh Aussie state, which they wanted to be known as Central Queensland. Apparently the seventh state movement began in the 1860s when Rockhampton residents took to the streets.

MANS CORNER

Image: John Hatwell

ICONOMETRE

7/10

We ain't got no beef with these Big Bulls.

one of the Big Bulls in Rocky

The BIG Cane Toad

Where it's at:

Sarina, 40 km south of **Mackay**.

Vitals:

DOB: 2004

Materials
papier-mâché and fibreglass

Aussies love an underdog, which is why 'Buffy the Big Cane Toad' will always have a place in our hearts. Built to attract tourists, this aesthetically-challenged amphibian has so far failed to pull in the punters. Could this be a result of its reputation as Australia's worst pest?

Rumour has it:

Nobody knows exactly how many cane toads there are in Australia but the number is definitely in the millions. The epidemic started in Queensland in 1932 when just 102 were introduced from Hawaii to control pests in the sugar cane plantations.

Did you know?

The name Buffy is derived from the scientific name for cane toads, 'bufo marinus', which is Latin for 'sea toad.'

Starring role:

Cane Toads – An Unnatural History is the hilarious 1988 BAFTA Award-nominated movie about the history of cane toads in Australia.

Anything else I should know?

In 2007 a group called FrogWatch, which aims to cull cane toads in the Northern Territory, caught one the size of a small dog. The heavy hopper weighed in at almost one kilogram but that's nothing compared to the world's biggest toad, which was 2.65kg.

Image: Sarina Tourist Art and Craft

The Big Cane Toad

4/10

The cane toad is arguably Australia's ugliest and most damaging feral species. But at least they're giving survival a fair go.

Where it's at:

Outside the Captain Cook Backpackers on Sheridan Street, which just happens to be along the Captain Cook Highway, **Cairns.**

Introducing...

The BIG Captain Cook

He was larger than life and he lived it to the full, so if anyone deserves to be turned into a Big Thing it has to be Captain James Cook. In many ways, Cook had all the attributes of a dinki-di Aussie battler - the son of a poor farmhand, he worked his guts out to become one of the world's most celebrated explorers.

Rumour has it:

Like all good 18th century seafarers, Big Captain Cook never left home without his big sextent. Regrettably it was nicked. Ironically, if the theft had happened 200 years ago, whoever was responsible might have found themselves transported here as a convict.

Did you know?

Probably the biggest misconception about Captain Cook is that he discovered Australia. While he did discover and claim Australia's east coast on behalf of British king, George III, the gong for the first European to walk on Aussie soil goes to Dutch explorer Dirk Hartog, who landed on the west coast in 1616.

Starring role:

We'll always remember Captain Cook. There are islands and a university named in his honour and there's even a Captain Cook Society, which was formed in 1975 and has members all over the world.

Anything else I should know?

While the paint on his breeches might need freshening up, the Big Captain Cook is unlikely to succumb to bad weather any time soon. Sculptor Chris Pigeon built him to survive a direct hit from a cyclone.

Image: Wikimedia Commons, Fosnez

The Big Captain Cook

Big it up for the Big Captain Cook.

The BIG Cassowary

Is it a bird, is it a plane ...? Actually yes, it is a bird, a giant Big Cassowary, no less. This docile-looking Big Thing is a monument to Australia's largest land animal, the Southern Cassowary, which grows up to 2m tall and can weigh 80kg.

Rumour has it:

The heads of all three species of cassowary are adorned with horn-like crests known as casques. Scientists aren't sure what they're for. Some reckon the casques act as crash helmets for when the birds are storming through the undergrowth. Others believe that cassowaries use them to generate a low frequency 'booming' sound in order to communicate.

Did you know?

Cassowaries are big flightless birds only found in northeast Australia and the island of New Guinea. Their three-toed feet have sharp claws, and the middle claw (which is about 12cm long) can be used to disembowel horses and humans.

Starring role:

The birds are so popular they even have their own awards. The Wet Tropics Management Authority presents the Cassowary Awards each year to individuals and groups who have made outstanding contributions to conservation.

Anything else I should know?

You can gawk at live cassowaries in the World Heritage listed rainforest that surrounds the Mission Beach area.

Image: Magda Peukert

ICONOMETRE

6/10

As a monument to one of the rainforests' most spectacular and endangered creatures, this concrete cassowary is a big reminder that we can never take nature for granted.

The Big Cassowary

Introducing...

The BIG Crab

Perched over the entrance to the Big Crab Restaurant, this colossal crustacean seems poised to pincer guests arriving for a seafood feast of local Mud Crabs. Luckily for us, the fiery red claws are only for show.

Rumour has it:

Counting the number of crab's legs can be confusing. Crabs have 10 legs. The confusion comes from the fact the front two have evolved as claws, which gives the impression that they only have eight legs.

Did you know?

There are 6793 crab species that we know about. The smallest is the pea crab, which is only a few millimetres wide, while the largest, the Japanese spider crab, has been reported to have a leg span of 4m.

Starring role:

What if the Big Crab came to life? This question, and more, was answered in the 1957 B-movie, *Attack of the Crab Monsters*. The catchy tagline for the film was: 'From the depths of the sea... a tidal wave of terror!'

Anything else I should know?

Every May, Cardwell commemorates the Coral Sea Battle, which was the first naval battle in history where enemy ships didn't come within sight of one another. The battle took place 800 kilometres off Cardwell's coast.

Image: Dave Hayes

The Big Crab

Introducing...

The BIG Dinosaur

Not even extinction could stop the Big Dinosaur getting its dues. Known to the boffins as Kronosaurus queenslandicus, this Big Thing is a re-creation of the fossil remains found in 1930 just 30 km north of Richmond.

Rumour has it:

While most fossil discoveries have been made elsewhere, Australia is a haven for fossil hunters. Some of the nation's best kept secrets are the locations of huge fossil deposits. At Lark Quarry near Winton, you can find the only remaining evidence of a dinosaur stampede: over 3000 footprints made by almost 200 dinosaurs more than 95 million years ago.

Did you know?

The 120 million year-old fossil remains of Kronosaurus were sent to Havard University, USA, where they were reassembled and put on display.

Starring role:

Dinosaurs hit the big screen in a whopping way with 1993 blockbuster *Jurassic Park* about a theme park featuring dinosaurs grown from genes found in fossilised remains.

Anything else I should know?

Kronosaurus fossils were first discovered in Queensland in 1889. They are the largest, and were probably the most ferocious of the ancient marine mammals called plesiosaurs. Kronosaurs had a strong sense of smell and massive jaws lined with rows of teeth the size of really big bananas.

Image: Megan Hussey - Kronosaurus Korner

ICONOMETRE

6/10

The Big Dinosaur stamps Aussie fossils on the map.

www.kronosauruskorner.com.au

The Big Dinosaur

Vitals:

DOB: 1992

Dimensions: 22m long, 12m wide, 5m high

Introducing...

The BIG Dugong

It's the Big Thing to represent the ocean's most loveable lumps. Dubbed 'sea cows' because they spend nearly all their time grazing gently on coastal beds of seagrass, dugongs are right up there with dolphins in the cute stakes.

Rumour has it:

The myth of mermaids came from ancient mariners mistaking dugongs and their Northen Hemisphere cousins, manatees, for women of the sea. The source of confusion was probably that dugong mothers, like humans, cuddle their babies in their arms.

Did you know?

Moreton Bay is the only spot anywhere in the world where dugongs hang out near a capital city. The population here is around 100,000 animals. To keep the herd together, the older males make whistling sounds so individual dugongs can keep their bearings.

Starring role:

In 2006, New Zealand recording artist Sharkweek released a single entitled 'The Dugong Song' although it's not clear what the connection is with the marine mammal.

Anything else I should know?

Real dugongs are nearly as large as the Big Dugong. They are known to grow to over 3m long and can weigh up to 400kg. They are also long-lived with a life expectancy of up to 70 years.

Image: David Joffe – Natureworks

ICONOMETRE

8/10

The Big Dugong is a reminder that Australia is one of the last safe-havens for dugongs in the wild.

The Big Dugong

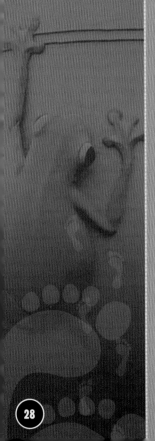

Introducing...

The BIG Gumboot

Whatever the weather, you can rely on the Big Gumboot to give you a grin. As you're gazing up at the giant gummie consider that its height is equivalent to the record annual rainfall that saturated the shire in 1950.

Rumour has it:

A friendly competition between Australia's three wettest towns, Tully, Babinda and Innisfail, led to a rubber boot being awarded each year to the town with the highest rainfall. Traditionally, Innisfail was always a strong contender until its rain gauge was moved away from the town's public toilets.

Did you know?

A gumboot is another name for Wellies or Wellington boots, which were named after Arthur Wellesley the 1st Duke of Wellington. The famous Duke, who in 1815 defeated Napoleon at the Battle of Waterloo, is credited with designing the world's original gummies.

Starring role:

Since 1985, the residents of Taihape in New Zealand have been amusing themselves with their yearly celebration of all things gumboot. The celebration, known as Gumboot Day, features a prize for best-dressed gumboot as well as a world-record attempt to set a new longest distance for gumboot throwing.

Anything else I should know?

Famous Aussie poet Henry Lawson, who was a contemporary of Banjo Paterson, wrote a poem about Blucher Boots in 1890. Blucher was a Prussian general who fought alongside Wellington at Waterloo. Apparently he also had a penchant for gummies.

Image: Wikimedia Commons, Frances76

GOLDEN GUMBOOT
TULLY · 'A PRETTY WET PLACE'
The height of the gumboot represents the amount of rainfall recorded in Tully in the year 1950 - 79 metres
The Australian Record

The Big Gumboot

5/10

By gum that Big Gumboot is gigantically good.

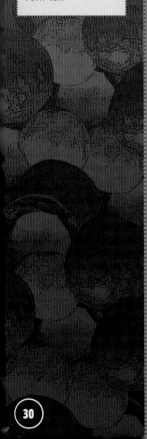

Introducing...

The BIG Macadamia Nut

Don't go off your nut, it's just a massive macadamia. Woombye's where the nutheads belong and here you can ride in the Macadamia Nutmobile or nibble on enough nutty snacks to turn you into a squirrel. The Big Macadamia is in the middle of a macadamia plantation, so bring your nutcracker and get stuck in.

Rumour has it:

Macadamias have the hardest shell of any nut. It takes 300 pounds per square inch of pressure to crack the shell and get to the tasty goodness inside.

Did you know?

The macadamia tree is native to Australia. In 1857 it was named after Dr John Macadam, an MP and Melbourne University chemistry professor who knew nothing about plants.

Starring role:

Believe it or not there is an Australian Macadamia Society whose 800 or so members represent all facets of the macadamia industry.

Anything else I should know?

Macadamias have gone green. The nut's hard shell burns almost as efficiently as coal and Gympie's newly opened Ergon Energy/Suncoast Gold Macadamia Nut Co-generation Plant (what a mouthful!) generates enough energy to power 1200 homes.

Image: Claire Garner

The Big Macadamia Nut

8/10

Let's hear it for an original Aussie nut job done good.

Where it's at:

The Golden Mile Orchard, **Mundubbera**, 390 km north-west of Brisbane.

Vitals:

DOB: 1983

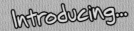

Introducing...

The BIG Mandarin

Heading into town from the coastal road, the Big Mandarin is a beacon intended to stamp Mundubbera's mandarin credentials on the map. Known by locals as the 'Enormous Ellendale' in reference to a popular mandarin variety, it will leave you in little doubt about the town's claims to be the Citrus Capital of Queensland.

Rumour has it:

Mandarin oranges are also widely known as tangerines. Native to South East Asia, the first mandarins to find their way to the English-speaking world were a couple of fruity fellas from Canton who arrived in England in 1805.

Did you know?

Vitamin C is the locals' lifeblood. The first citrus trees were planted here in the 1890s and by the 1980s the region produced nearly all of Australia's mandarin exports. Today, the Golden Mile Orchard is the Southern Hemisphere's biggest single citrus orchard.

Starring role:

Mandarins are prized by doctors of Chinese medicine who use them to treat insomnia, and skin and digestive problems.

Anything else I should know?

Mandarin essential oil is an important active ingredient in many expensive floral perfumes and colognes. Mandarins destined to be used in the scent industry are produced in Italy, Sicily and Algiers.

Image: Simon Brown

ICONOMETRE

4/10

It's no coincidence that marvellous, magnificent and mandarin all begin with a Big M.

The Big Mandarin

The BIG Mango

Where it's at:

Located on the Bruce Highway, 4 km south of **Bowen**, overlooking Edgecumbe Bay.

Vitals:

DOB: 2002

Dimensions: 12m high

Mad-for-it mango-munchers will recognise that this is no ordinary fruit. It is a monument to the variety proudly known as Kensington Pride, which is so popular it makes up over 80 per cent of all mango trees planted in Australia.

Rumour has it:

The Kensington Pride variety was officially discovered in Bowen but is thought to have originated as a seed imported on a ship that sailed here from India. The Big Mango is upside down compared with how mangoes normally hang from trees.

Did you know?

The Guiness World Record for the mightiest mango goes to Hawaiian orchard farmer Colleen Porter, whose 2.5kg fruit was bigger than her head.

Starring role:

Marvellous mangoes are celebrated in festivals around the world. At the annual International Mango Festival in Delhi, India, growers showcase an amazing 550 mango varieties.

Anything else I should know?

Bowen is seriously mango mad. The Big Mango is where you'll find the town's tourist information centre, which stocks a disturbing amount of Mango-themed souvenirs, preserves, snacks and drinks, plus locally made mango-flavoured ice cream.

Image: Wikimedia Commons, Amos T Fairchild

9/10

A massive mango on a road called the Bruce Highway? Streuth, mate, if it was any more Australian it would have to be ridin' a dingo.

The Big Mango

Where it's at:

Outside Yatala Pies' new shop in **Yatala**, about halfway between Brisbane and the Gold Coast. Take the Yatala North turnoff and ignore the signs for MacDonalds.

Vitals:

DOB: 1999

Dimensions: 4.5m diameter

Introducing...

The BIG Pie

This Big Thing might well be an airy-fairy pie in the sky, but it is also a sure sign that your taste buds are in for one heck of a top treat. Mounted like a UFO atop a totem pole, the Big Pie is a grand advert for famous Yatala Pies, which have been sustaining Queenslanders for over 60 years.

Rumour has it:

According to experts it's pretty obvious who ate all the pies. On average each Australian puts away 12 pies every year.

Did you know?

Ancient Romans are believed to have invented pies when they came up with the idea of using flour and water paste to seal in meaty cooked juices.

Starring role:

A jingle for a 1970s Holden TV commercial attempted to link Holden motor vehicles with other Australian icons: football, kangaroos, and meat pies.

Anything else I should know?

To have the ultimate pie-x-perience you don't even have to leave the car. Simply cruise past the Big Pie into the drive-thru section, pick up your pie, and pack it down as you peel off along the Gold Coast Motorway.

Image: Wikimedia Commons/The Pom

The Big Pie

7/10

In 2003 former New South Wales Premier Bob Carr described meat pies as Australia's national dish.

The BIG Pineapple

Where it's at:

On the Nambour Connection Road at **Woombye** about 90 minutes north of Brisbane.

Vitals:

DOB: 1971

Dimensions: 16m high

One of the earliest Big Things to grace the Aussie landscape, the Big Pineapple is a fruity fanfare to the South American native that feels right at home in tropical Queensland.

Rumour has it:

Pine cones used to be called pineapples. When Europeans discovered pineapples, the South American fruit, they called them pineapples because they looked similar to what we now know as pine cones. The name 'pine cone' was only introduced in 1694 to avoid the confusion that came from calling two different things by the same name.

Did you know?

Lyn and Bill Taylor constructed the Big Pineapple less than a year after buying the 23-hectare pineapple farm running along the coastal side of the Bruce Highway. The plantation has since changed hands many times, and this Big Thing has survived ups and downs including a fire and a tornado.

Starring role:

Pineapples feature in quite a few adult jokes (ask Mum and Dad if you're not an adult) so it's no surprise the guys who made *Superbad* finally got around to shooting a film called *Pineapple Express* about a less than ideal series of events.

Anything else I should know?

If you ever have trouble digesting your food, gobble a pineapple. Apparently they contain the enzyme bromelain that can help your body break down other foods.

Image: Wikimedia Commons, Baycha Byrne

The Big Pineapple

10/10!

The National Trust of Queensland declared the Big Pineapple a national icon and who are we to argue?

The BIG Redback Spider

It's an arachnophobe's worst nightmare but to us, the Big Redback seems kind of cute in a giant, deadly kinda way. The epic-sized arachnid clambers over a backyard toilet as a reminder of the old outdoor dunnies, when over 80 per cent of Redback bites occurred when victims were in the act of 'relieving' themselves.

Rumour has it:

In April 2008, the Baralaba Hospital in central Queensland had to close while fumigators exterminated Redbacks that had infested the wards. Apparently, the spiders were seeking refuge from the drought-breaking deluges that had flooded the state.

Did you know?

Every year, over 250 doses of antivenom are given to people who've been bitten by a Redback. Luckily, it's only the female bite that's dangerous or there would be double the peril.

Starring role:

Aussie country music legend Slim Newton had a number one hit with his first ever recording *Redback on the Toilet Seat*. The year was 1971 and Slim was 39.

Anything else I should know?

Redbacks belong to the spider family Theridiidae, which is found all over the world.

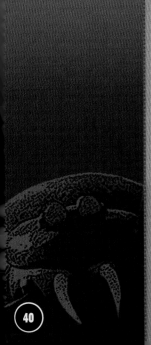

Image: David Joffe, Natureworks

ICONOMETRE

9/10

Redbacks rank in the top 10 of Australia's deadliest creatures, so the Big Redback definitely gets our respect.

The Big Redback Spider

The BIG Stubby

Where it's at:

Outside the House of Bottles, **Tewantin**.

Vitals:

DOB: 1966

Dimensions:
9m high, 4m wide

Materials:
stubbies

Chuck away the bricks and break out your bottles. The Big Stubby is the jewel in the crown of bottled treasures at the inspirational House of Bottles. And if, in a moment of madness, you think you've had enough of Big Things, then head over to the Wee Stubby – the toddler-sized version for kids.

Rumour has it:

Beer connoisseurs believe the major benefit of stubbies is that they allow the dedicated drinker to sink the contents easier and without causing excess foam and spillage.

Did you know?

A stubby is the name given to short glass beer bottles, which were designed to aid easier transportation.

Starring role:

Stubby was the name of a famous dog during World War I. After being smuggled to France by US soldier Corporal Robert Conroy, Stubby saved his human comrades by sniffing out a German spy lurking in the trenches. The terrier-cross was awarded a 'wound stripe' after being injured by a grenade and even 'shook hands' with President Woodrow Wilson.

Anything else I should know?

Just about everything on display at the House of Bottles is built from bottles. Five thousand were used to construct the toilets and the house itself used 14,000. Of course, the Big Stubby needed the most – an impressive 17,000. The question is, who emptied them first?

Image: AAP

The Big Stubby

9/10

Australians didn't invent the stubby but we did invent the stubby cooler so we can all drink with pride.

The Big Axe

The Big Banana

The Big Mushroom

The Big Golden Guitar

The Big Oyster

The Big

The Big Chook

The Big Prawn

The Big Avocado

New South Wales & ACT

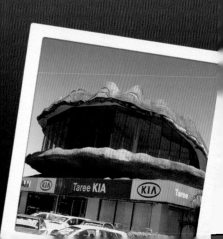

Where it's at:

Outside Tropical Fruit World on the Duranbah Road in between **Tumbulgum** and **Duranbah**.

Vitals:

DOB: 1983

Introducing...

The BIG Avocado

You have arrived at the centre of avocado activity in Australia. The adventure park advertised by the Big Avocado used to be called Avocado Adventureland but it was so popular that the other fruits wanted in on the action. Tropical Fruit World now hosts a safari and over 500 fruits.

Rumour has it:

The Aztecs of Mexico invented the word avocado, which in the Nahuatl language means 'testicle'. For this reason, perhaps, avocados have a reputation as being a fertility fruit.

Did you know?

People have been gorging on avos for longer than anyone can remember. In Mexico, scientists believe they've found evidence that avocado cultivation has been going on for more than 10,000 years.

Starring role:

Cannibal Women in the Avocado Jungle of Death is a bizarre 1989 B-movie about how far the US government will go in order to protect the world's avocado supplies.

Anything else I should know?

Can't shake that cold? Then indulge in avocado. The feisty fruit contains bucket-loads of vitamins and zinc, which is a stimulant for your immune system.

Image: Tropical Fruit World

4/10

Avos have been part of the Australian farming landscape since 1928, which makes them practically part of the family.

The Big Avocado

Introducing... The BIG Axe

Where it's at:

At a rest stop along the Pacific Highway, not far from **Kew**.

Vitals:

DOB: 2002

Dimensions: 8m-long handle

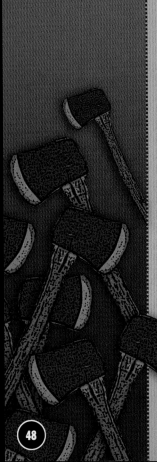

Is that a giant axe over the entrance to the car park, or are the residents of Duranbah just pleased to see you? Vehicles venturing up the north coast are advised to visit Kew where you can gaze up at the Big Axe, big enough for the likes of Godzilla or King Kong.

Rumour has it:

Our ancient ancestors were pretty keen on the old axe, but it wasn't only us that used them. Archaeologists have found evidence of hand axes up to 1.6 million years old. It is believed they belonged to early humans as well as our extinct cousins, Homo-Erectus.

Did you know?

Among the crucial equipment and supplies that arrived in Australia with the First Fleet were 700 felling axes. From the day they went ashore in 1789, male convicts used them to clear trees for the new settlement at Sydney Cove.

Starring role:

Gimli, the Dwarf in Lord of the Rings, raised the status of axes across the realm by wielding a double-handed battleaxe. Hardcore fans are able to buy replicas of Gimli's axe in two sizes. Apparently, they make a great addition to the Gimli costume.

Anything else I should know?

The original Big Axe was erected as a tribute to local champion axeman, Mannie McCarthy, who won over 20 world championships and was apparently still chopping wood at the age of 77.

Image: Dave Phillips

The Big Axe

Introducing...

The BIG Banana

The original, and as many would argue, still the best. Since it first appeared by the roadside over half a century ago, the Big Banana has gone big business. In 1989, the Big Banana reopened as a whole world of adventure after a $30 million redevelopment.

Rumour has it:

Bananas have been a hit for millennia. The first mention of a banana is in an ancient Buddhist text that dates from 600BC. The word banana was taken from the Arabic word for 'finger.'

Did you know?

The big legend of the Big Banana began back in the swinging sixties. John Landy had set up a roadside banana stall and needed a way to get the attention of oncoming traffic. And what better sign than a great Big Thing? He gave the builders his best-looking banana as a model and on December 22, 1964, Australia's first Big Thing was unveiled.

Starring role:

Probably the most famous bananas are the ones dressed for bed. *Bananas in Pyjamas* is an internationally famous kids' TV show produced by the ABC and stars two nutty nanas named B1 and B2.

Anything else I should know?

Go bananas in the gift shop and café where you can pick up everything from banana water pistols to frozen banana snacks.

THE BIG **BANANA**
COFFS HARBOUR

Celebrating 40 Years

Image: Wikimedia Commons, Paulscf

ICONOMETRE

The Big Banana

10/10!

The Big Banana has spawned a whole bunch of over 150 Big Things. If it weren't for this Big Thing, we might be living in a world of small to medium-sized things, and then where would we be?

The BIG Blue Heeler

Go barking mad for the bashful beauty of the Big Blue Heeler. Named 'Hunter' by local school kids, the mighty mutt is a monument to the farm dogs that supported the region's economy for over 150 years.

Rumour has it:

Blue Heelers are a breed of Australian cattle dog originally used to control wayward herds. The breed was established by 1897 but its origins are a bit murky. Heelers are believed to be the result of cross-breeding with collies, dingoes, and a bite-size of bull terrier.

Did you know?

An Australian cattle dog holds the record for the oldest canine that ever lived. 'Bluey' lived to be 29 in human years – that's 203 in dog years.

Starring role:

Blue Heelers was a popular Seven Network police drama about the lives of rural coppers in a Victorian country town. We think the producers missed an opportunity by not setting it in Muswellbrook.

Anything else I should know?

Known for their reliability, intelligence, and endurance, blue heelers are one of the hardest working dogs in the world. They're also among the most popular, consistently ranking in Australia's Top 10 of most popular breeds.

Image: Dave Hayes

The Big Blue Heeler

ICONOMETRE

8/10

Dogs are our best friends, and we couldn't think of a more p-awsome Big Thing than the Big Blue Heeler.

Introducing...

The BIG Chook

Cross the road and cluck your heart out dancing the 'funky chicken' in front of this giant feathered favourite – the Big Chook. This big thing has proved popular despite not looking like any chicken we've ever seen. I wonder if it lays eggs?

Rumour has it:

Scientists believe chickens are the closest living relatives to *Tyrannosaurus rex*, the most feared dinosaur of its day. The link was made by analysing collagen protein found in the fossilised leg bone of a T. Rex that died 68 million years ago.

Did you know?

Australia loves chicken. Each year around 450 million cluckers are killed for their meat. The poultry industry is worth over $1.3 billion.

Starring role:

Which came first, the chicken or the egg? It's the world's greatest conundrum and it is still unanswered. In 2006, a boffin at King's College, London, claimed to have solved the mystery by saying the first chicken had to hatch from an egg. But then the question remains, if a chicken didn't lay the egg, what did?

Anything else I should know?

Chickens were important passengers on board the First Fleet. Along with geese, ducks, turkeys, and wildfowl, there were 87 chickens hoping to start a new life in Australia.

Image: Penrith Valley Visitor Centre

ICONOMETRE

5/10

Crow me a river - the Big Chook is finger lickin' good.

The Big Chook

Where it's at:

As you ride up to **Tamworth** along the New England Highway.

Vitals:

DOB: 1988

Dimensions: 12m high, weighs 0.5 tonnes

Materials: fibreglass over a steel frame

Introducing...

The BIG Golden Guitar

Welcome ya'll to the home of country music. Forget Nashville, Tennessee. Tamworth, NSW is where the action's at and the Big Golden Guitar is here to prove it.

Rumour has it:

Around the world, America is known as the birthplace of country music, but Australia's rural music traditions hark back to the 1800s with the bush balladeers who sang about life, love, and living without luxury in the bush.

Did you know?

Slim Dusty is remembered as the grand-daddy of Aussie country music, and it was he who unveiled the Big Golden Guitar when he was in his sixties. Slim's career began in the 1940s, lasted half a century, and saw him record over 100 albums.

Starring role:

Every year around 50,000 country fans flock to Tamworth for the annual music festival. And just about every one of them gets their picture taken next to the Big Golden Guitar.

Anything else I should know?

The Big Golden Guitar is modelled on the Golden Guitar awards handed out at the Country Music Association of Australia Awards. The first Golden Guitar went to Slim Dusty's wife Joy McKean in 1972.

Image: Wikimedia Commons, Rod Edwards

oldenguitar.com.au

TAMWORTH

ICONOMETRE

10/10!

Viva Tam-vegas and let the good times roll with the Big Golden Guitar.

The Big Golden Guitar

Introducing...
The BIG Joint

Roll up, roll up and take your seats around this beefy bifta. The Big Joint is one of the few Big Things to have sparked genuine controversy, which is hardly surprising seeing as joints, or rather what's in them, is illegal.

Rumour has it:

It's believed that the first people to get high on marijuana lived in India around 1000 BC. Hindu culture is peppered with references to cannabis resin although recent studies have linked heavy use with schizophrenia.

Did you know?

The Big Joint is mobile and makes irregular forays to support pro-cannabis protests around the country. In 2000, Victoria Police 'arrested' the colossal cannabis cone from demonstrators outside the Crown Casino in Melbourne. In 2006, just after the Nimbin Mardi Gras, protestors drove it to Canberra and rebuilt it outside Parliament House.

Starring role:

Pot smokers often fantasise about smoking ridiculously oversized joints, which might explain where the idea for the Big Joint came from. In 2006, a group from Amsterdam planned to roll and smoke a 1.5m-long joint using half a kilo of marijuana. The plan was shelved when they realised using so much skunk would make it illegal, even in Holland.

Anything else I should know?

A survey for the Australian Institute of Health and Welfare showed that 39 per cent of Australians admitted using cannabis at least once. Nearly 20 per cent had smoked a joint within the past year.

Image: Hemp Embassy

The Big Joint

ICONOMETRE

7/10

Smokin'.

The BIG Merino

Where it's at:

Goulburn, if you take the southern exit of the Hume Expressway.

The Big Merino is a giant monument to the sheep with the softest, smoothest, and finest wool of any breed. The radiant ram, nicknamed Rambo, is a true work of art and its detailed design has been known to make sheep shearers weak at the knees.

Rumour has it:

'Merino' is a Spanish word that supposedly comes from the name of a Castilian sheep inspector who fastidiously inspected the shepherds' flocks.

Did you know?

Englishman John Macarthur brought the first flock of Merinos to Australia in 1804. Although he returned home to Blighty the following year, he is still regarded as the founder of the Aussie Merino industry, which today produces almost 80 per cent of the world's Merino wool.

Starring role:

Black Sheep was the title of the 2006 NZ comedy about genetically engineered killer sheep on the rampage.

Anything else I should know?

In 2007, changes to the Goulburn bi-pass meant the massive Merino had to be moved 800m to its current spot. Not an easy task when you consider 'Rambo' weighs more than 21 average-sized Merino rams.

Image: Wikimedia Commons, Itsgrimupnorth

The Big Merino

ICONOMETRE

7/10

While shepherds watch their flocks at night it must be comforting to know the Big Merino is looking out for them.

Vitals:

Dimensions:
6m tall with
a diameter of
15.6m, covering a
total area of 190
sqm.

Introducing...

The BIG Mushroom

Maybe the ACT is trying to send the rest of the country a message by having only one Big Thing to its credit. Luckily, the Big Mushroom doubles as an adventure playground so it's a hit with the kids, otherwise it may not have warranted a mention at all and the ACT would have been written off the Big Things Map. Not that anyone there seems to care.

Rumour has it:
When it comes to being massive, mushrooms could eat a whale for breakfast. The largest living organism ever discovered is the *Armillaria ostoyae*, known as the honey mushroom, which covers 880 square hectares of the Malheur National Forest in Oregon, USA. It has been growing for around 2400 years.

Did you know?
Mushrooms might be more at home on the dinner plate, but they are not vegetables. They are the fruiting body of a fungus.

Starring role:
In 2007, a 100 million year-old mushroom made headlines around the world following its discovery embedded in a fossilised piece of amber.

Anything else I should know?
You may find it hard to believe, but the Big Mushroom is the only mushroom adventure playground in Australia. We know what you're thinking. Why, when this one is so much fun?

Image: John Hatwell

The Big Mushroom

Where it's at:

The tasteful town of **Taree**, 317 km north-east of Sydney.

Vitals:

DOB:
The Big Oyster miraculously appeared in the early nineties. Not even the Taree Council Planning Department knows the exact date.

Introducing...
The BIG Oyster

Like the Big Prawn at Ballina, the Big Oyster started life as the shell of a restaurant, which has since shut down. But just because it's no longer in use doesn't make it any less tacky or spectacular. Indeed, the fact that it no longer serves any functional purpose makes this Big Thing seem even more iconic.

Rumour has it:

Casanova, the legendary Italian stallion, is said to have started each day with a banquet of oysters so he'd have enough energy for the night's inevitable activities.

Did you know?

Oysters are a type of mollusc and have been around since the Triassic Period 200 million years ago. Middens across Australia show that Aborigines enjoyed eating fresh oysters for centuries before Europeans arrived.

Starring role:

The Big Oyster: History on the Half Shell is a fascinating history of, ah, you guessed. it. Go on, become an oyster expert.

Anything else I should know?

Taree is the resting place of the Big Oyster and it's name comes from the Aboriginal 'tareebit' – the word for a local fig tree.

Image: Wikimedia Commons - Stuart Edwards

Taree KIA   KIA   Taree

ICONOMETRE

6/10

A Big Thing honouring the world's most famous and tested aphrodisiac is an essential part of the Big Things landscape.

The Big Oyster

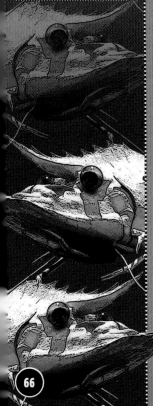

Where it's at:

The Big Prawn is the first thing you'll notice as you come into the township of **Ballina**, 753 km north of Sydney.

Vitals:

DOB: 1989

Dimensions:
27m long, 20m high, 4.5m wide

Introducing...
The BIG Prawn

Prawnies, meaning people who fish for prawns, will instantly recognise Ballina's Big Prawn as being of the Tiger variety. Hugging the top of the restaurant and souvenir shop complex, the sizeable shrimp looks as if it knows it's about to be pan-fried and served with garlic.

Rumour has it:

The viewing platform at the top of the stairs had to be closed because of the increased cost of public liability insurance.

Did you know?

Scientists have unearthed a 390 million year old fossil of a gigantic killer prawn. The 2.5 metre-long monster used 46cm claws to dice up its prey before devouring it with the multiple mouths lining its stomach.

Starring role:

It was a prawn, not a shrimp, that Paul Hogan was referring to in the 1980s TV adverts that gave us the phrase 'slip another shrimp on the barbie.' Even though most Aussies use the word prawn, the TV executives changed it to shrimp so as not to confuse the audience in the USA, where the adverts were screened.

Anything else I should know?

Even though the prawn industry is big business in Ballina, local residents lodged over 160 complaints when the Big Prawn was proposed.

Image: Wikimedia Commons; Stuart Edwards

ICONOMETRE

8/10

Two thumbs up from us because you can't get any tackier than the Big Prawn.

The Big Prawn

The BIG Wine Cask

Where it's at:

BRL Stanley winery at **Buronga**, along the Silver City Highway.

Vitals:

DOB: 1983

Dimensions: 8m high, 11m long, 7m wide.

You don't have to be a wino to appreciate the whopping 400,000-litre capacity of the Big Wine Cask. While knocking back this cask's contents might be a dream come true for some, most visitors are content to sample more manageable quantities of plonk from the adjacent BRL Stanley winery.

Rumour has it:

Thomas 'Tom' Angrove invented the wine cask and patented the design in 1965. It's thought the idea for the invention came when he saw a Greek shepherd drinking from a goatskin.

Did you know?

The wine cask took two years to develop and its original name was 'improved container and pack for liquids.' The first wines to be sold were table white, table red, port, sweet sherry and muscat. Aussies took the cask to heart and gave it the nickname 'Chateau Cardboard.'

Starring role:

Wine has played a pivotal role in Australia since the early 19th century. In 1814, an ex-convict named Dr Redfern was asked by Governor Macquarie to establish why so many convicts were dying quickly after arrival. Dr Redfern insisted all convicts should be given a pint of wine a day to prevent scurvy and malnutrition. Thanks to wine, many lives were saved.

Anything else I should know?

Campers should note that a wine cask's empty bladder can be easily inflated for use as a pillow.

Image: Tony Allen

10/10!

Even posh girls love a cask.

The Big Wine Cask

The Big Wool Bales

the Big Wave

...ray Cod

The Big Worm

The Big Koala

The Big Ned

The Big Koala

The Big Strawberry

The Big Murray Cod

Victoria

The Big Wool Bales

The Big L

The BIG Koala

If Australia's favourite animal was anywhere near the size of the Big Koala, then it might not have quite the same reputation for being so cute and cuddly. At a whopping 14m high, its official name is Giant Koala, or Mr Koala, sir. Inside the mammoth marsupial is a gift shop and cafe, which proves it's always handy to know what a koala keeps in its pouch.

Rumour has it:

While it might look like a cuddly little bear, the koala is no such thing. They are marsupials, and just like kangaroos and wombats, the females carry their young in a pouch.

Did you know?

Koalas are found only in Australia and their name comes from an Aboriginal word meaning 'no drink', as the ancient Aborigines saw that Koalas get all their fluids through eating eucalyptus leaves.

Starring role:

In the 1981 animated film *Toby and the Koala Bear*, a koala helps his young friend Toby escape from a convict settlement.

Anything else I should know?

Koalas spend most of the time sleeping and are only really active for around two hours each day. On average they spend 75 per cent of their lives asleep.

Image: Wikimedia Commons, Bilby

GIANT KOALA
Tourist complex

The Big Koala

9/10

An icon animal for Australia, what we like about this Big Thing is that any attempt to get up close and personal could result in a nasty 'gravel rash', which is a bit like what would happen if you tried to cuddle the real thing.

The BIG Murray Cod

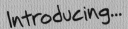

Where it's at:

Next to the railway station on Curlewis Street in **Swan Hill.**

Vitals:

DOB: 1992

Dimensions: 11m long and 6m wide

Well, batter me lightly and serve me with chips. The first time you happen to cross the marvellous Big Murray Cod, you'll be struck by its outstanding natural beauty. For a statue of a fish it really is rather fetching, which probably has a lot to do with how it came into being, and even more to do with the magnificence of the fish on which it was modelled.

Rumour has it:

The Boorong Aborigines call Murray Cod, 'Otchocut', which is represented by the stars of the Delphinus (dolphin) constellation. The disappearance of the Otchocut's stars from the night sky during September and October coincides with the end of the spawning season.

Did you know?

Murray cod are the largest freshwater fish in Australia. The biggest one ever recorded was 183cm long and weighed 113kg. That's a lot of fish and chips.

Starring role:

The mighty Murray Cod was built as a prop for the 1992 movie *Eight Ball*. After the film crew left, locals were so rapt with the fish they found it a permanent home.

Anything else I should know?

Since Europeans arrived, the Murray Cod has declined rapidly and is no longer common in many parts of the Murray Basin.

Image: Wikimedia Commons, Mattinbgn

The Big Murray Cod

ICONOMETRE

8/10

No other fish species symbolises conservation like the Murray Cod, so this Big Thing stands for something even bigger than itself.

The BIG Ned

Where it's at:

Glenrowan, near where Victorian Police finally caught up with the Kelly gang.

Vitals:

DOB: 1992

Dimensions: 6m tall

Materials: Fibreglass

No other character is so ingrained in the Australian psyche as bushranger and convicted murderer Edward 'Ned' Kelly. Big Ned rises up wearing the suit of armour that guaranteed him a place in the history books and our imaginations, forever.

Rumour has it:

After Ned Kelly was captured he was put on trial at Melbourne's Old Gaol. He was found guilty of murdering a policeman and as he went to the gallows his last words are thought to have been, 'Such is life.' He was hanged on 11 November 1880.

Did you know?

This is the third incarnation of Big Ned. The first was stolen and found floating in a river, the second was relocated to inside the Kellyland Museum. This version was built by the owners of Kate's Cottage – Rod and Chris Gerrett.

Starring role:

Ned Kelly was the star of the world's first ever feature film, *The Story of the Kelly Gang* made in 1906.

Anything else I should know?

The real Ned Kelly probably could have escaped capture at Glenrowan but sealed his fate when he went back to rescue two of his gang who were already fatally wounded.

Image: Wikimedia Commons, Bilb...wan 3676

Image: Genevieve Bel

The Big Ned

10/10!

Whatever your opinion of Ned Kelly's actions, the man himself deserves respect. In the siege at Glenrowan, 28 bullets, slugs and shotgun pellets hit him, yet he still survived.

Where it's at:

On the edge of the car park at the Scenic Drive Strawberry Farm in **Koonoomoo**, 264 km north of Melbourne.

Vitals:

DOB: March 2005

Dimensions: 4.5m high, 3m wide

Materials: 540m of wrapped steel covered in fibreglass

Introducing...

The BIG Strawberry

The sun is shining, the birds are singing... break out your punnets and get strawberry picking. The Big Strawberry is one of the juiciest new delights on the Big Things map. The best bit is that it lives on a strawberry farm where you can pick your own and slurp them down to your heart's content.

Rumour has it:

Even though its fruit is covered in seeds, strawberry plants grow by sending out runners that develop into new plants. Hence the word strawberry is believed to originate from the Saxon word 'strew', meaning 'to spread around', and 'berry', meaning fruit.

Did you know?

Strawberries, apples, and apricots, along with roses and plums, are all part of the Rosaceae family.

Starring role:

Every September, Moreton Bay holds its annual Leisure Life Spring Festival, the highlight of which is its famous strawberry-eating contest. Under 12s battle it out in the 100g category while the olds munch to glory in the 250g Open Final.

Anything else I should know?

Can't remember stuff? Eat a strawberry. In 2006, researchers at the Salk Institute for Biological Studies reported that fisetin, a substance found in strawberries and other fruits and vegetables, can improve memory by stimulating the brain's signalling pathways.

Image: Wikimedia Commons, Mattinbgn

6/10

People who treat their bodies as temples will appreciate this monument to the jewel of the fruity kingdom.

The Big Strawberry

The BIG Wave

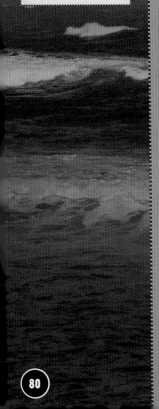

San Remo, near Phillip Island, outside, you guessed it, a surf shop.

Vitals:

DOB: 1993

Dimensions: 3m high and 5m long

Materials: ferro-concrete

This is exactly the sort of epic, hollow tube-ride surfers have wet dreams about and now it's here, cast in concrete to allow even the most unbalanced malco to experience surfing's ultimate thrill. Pull into the car park, pull out your camera, and snap your loved one, or brother, sister, Mum and Dad pulling Hang Ten deep inside the barrel. It really is more fun than it should be.

Rumour has it:

The town's name was changed to San Remo in 1888 and named after the popular tourist spot on the Italian Riviera.

Did you know?

The first world surfing championship was a one-day event held at Manly in Sydney. The year was 1964 and the winner was Aussie longboard legend Midget Farrelly.

Starring role:

Probably the most famous surfing sequence captured on film is the scene at the end of the movie *Point Break* where Cody (Patrick Swayze) is killed by a once-in-thirty-years swell. Bizarrely, the wipe-out was filmed at Waimea Beach in Hawaii. Guess the Aussie waves were too gnarly!

Anything else I should know?

Australia has had an incredible 22 surfing world champions, including some record-breaking individual efforts. Layne Beachley has taken the women's title 7 times, while Mark Richards and Nat Young took the men's shortboard and longboard titles 5 and 4 times each.

Image: Scott Jackson

The Big Wave

7/10

Where would Australia be without surfing and where would surfing be without Australia? Luckily these are questions we shall never have to ask, because surfing is an icon of Aussie culture with its own Big Thing to prove it.

Where it's at:

Just west of **Hamilton** along Coleraine Road on the Henty Highway.

Vitals:

DOB: 1989

Dimensions: 10m long and 7m wide

Introducing...

The BIG Wool Bales

You'll be 'baled' over for sure when you step inside the five Big Wool Bales. Local shearers are on hand to give hands-on demonstrations of their sheep-shearing technique. And while some city slickers might think it all sounds a bit country-bumpkin style, we guarantee that after you've seen these boys in action you'll have a newfound respect for the origins of your favourite knitwear.

What is it exactly?

A wool bale can refer to either a container for raw wool, as in the case of the Big Wool Bales, or a standard-sized pack of mechanically packed wool.

Did you know?

It takes around 60 fleeces to fill a wool bale, depending on the size and age of the sheep.

Starring role:

In 2001, Aussie sheep breeders Ed and Jill Hundy won the first World Record Wool Challenge Cup for wool bales. The prize was judged and awarded in Rome, Italy, and the winning bale contained enough high-quality wool to make 50 of the finest Italian suits.

BIG WOOLBA
HAMILTON - VICTORIA - AU
WOOL CAPITAL OF THE
WOOL DISPLAYS   LIGH
SHEARING DEMO'S

BIG WOOL BALES Cafe

WOOL BALES
SHEARING
SUPPLIES
PH: 5571 2810

Gift Shop
Souvenirs

Image: Genevieve Bell

The Big Wool Bales

5/10

There are roughly 120 million sheep in Australia, which means there probably needs to be quite a few wool bales. And to all those bales, the five Big Wool Bales salute you.

The BIG Worm

Healthy people need to eat healthy crops, and healthy crops need healthy soil, which makes the real-life star of this Big Thing a friend to us all. The Big Worm is loosely modelled on the world's largest species, the Giant Gippsland Earthworm. While the real worms are usually pinkish purple, the Big Worm is painted with Indigenous art.

Rumour has it:

Stamp near a Giant Gippsland Earthworm's nest and you'll hear one of the weirdest sounds in nature. As they slide through their escape tunnels, the worms make a gurgling sound because of a special fluid they use to keep the chambers slippery.

Did you know?

Southern Gippsland is the only place on Earth you'll find these giant fellas who can grow up to 4m long – if you stretch them out.

Starring role:

Bizarrely, the country's most famous worm can be spotted on TV around the time of federal elections. Since 1993 'The Worm' has been used to measure audience reactions to debating prime ministerial candidates.

Anything else I should know?

Giant Gippsland Earthworms are facing extinction due to increased farming on its traditional habitat. If you ever find one, don't pick it up, as handling by humans usually spells the end for the long pink behemoths.

Image: Wildlife Wonderland

ICONOMETRE

7/10

A big worm in a paddock? Now there's an icon for ya.

The Big Worm

The Big Scotsman

The Big Miner

ange

The Big Kangaroo

The Big Miner

CE'S BAKERY

The Big Rock

The Big Scotsman

The Big Rocking Horse

The Big Lobster

The Big Scotsman

South Australia

...roo

The Big Galah

The BIG Galah

Where it's at:

Right next to the **Eyre Highway**, beside Kimba's wheat silos.

Vitals:

DOB: 21 July 1993

Dimensions: 8m tall and weighs over 2 tonnes

Materials: Steel, fibreglass and bird wire

Gawking at the Big Galah is a popular pastime if you're passing through Kimba. The tiny town, population 1300, is almost exactly midway between the east and west coasts. It's no coincidence, then, that you'll find the big bird perched in front of the Halfway Across Australia Gem Shop.

Rumour has it:

Bird watchers have reported seeing galahs flying into whirlwinds for fun. There has even been a report of a whole flock of galahs launching themselves into a tornado, which immediately spat them out screeching with delight.

Did you know?

The land where Kimba now stands was discovered by the explorer Edward John Eyre who, with the help of an Aboriginal boy named Wylie, became the first European to cross the Nullarbor in 1840-41.

Starring role:

Alf Stewart from *Home and Away* made the phrase 'flamin' galah' internationally famous by using it whenever someone upset him.

Anything else I should know?

Another name for galahs is the rose-breasted cockatoo. The word galah comes from 'gilaa', which is a Yuwaalaray Aboriginal word. A typical flesh and blood galah is only about 35cm long and weighs 400g, which makes the Big Galah about 23 times larger than life.

Image: Wikimedia Commons, Adam Eales

The Big Galah

8/10

The road crossing the Nullarbor can get pretty tedious so it's a welcome sight to see this great pink and grey galah. Not only is the Big Galah a huge tourist attraction, it's a travel icon too.

The BIG Kangaroo

Where it's at:

Opposite the Border Village truck stop on the Eyre Highway, about 1200 km from Adelaide.

Vitals:

DOB: 1986

Dimensions: 5m tall

Materials: polystyrene, papier-mâché, and fibreglass.

Rooey II is Australia's biggest Kangaroo. Overlooking the highway from its concrete plinth just outside Border Village, the big red 'roo holds out a can of soft drink to entice travellers to pull over for a break.

Rumour has it:

Apparently, the mighty marsupial used to hold a can of beer but politically-correct locals decided that this was the wrong message to send out. It now holds a popular brand of soft drink, which has led to suggestions it's a marketing ploy.

Did you know?

The name Rooey II was chosen from entries to a local competition to give the Big Thing its name. It was supposed to be Ruey II but the sign writer, who goes by the name Saltbrush Bill, misspelt it.

Starring role:

Skippy. Need we say more?

Anything else I should know?

The truck store owners, Allan Schwarz and Brian Rucioch, originally wanted a Big Matilda – mascot of the 1982 Brisbane Commonwealth Games. At the time, Matilda was on a world tour so they decided to build their own version instead.

Image: Pete Johns

The Big Kangaroo

ICONOMETRE

9/10

Let's face it — you can't get much more iconic than a giant 'roo. What's strange is that it took until the late 1980s for somebody to turn one into a Big Thing.

The BIG Lobster

Where it's at:
Kingston, South Australia, 300 km from Adelaide.

Vitals:
Dimensions:
At 18 m tall and 4 tonnes in weight, it's a whole lotta lobster

Materials:
Not sure, but it's not edible

How's this for a pose? Raised up on its tail with its claws poised as if in mid-attack, this 8-legged, 2-clawed behemoth would make you run a mile if it wasn't for the friendly pink paint-job that screams out, 'Hey, I just want to be friends.' Unlike some of our iconic Big Things, this lofty lobster is remarkably well-maintained. Make sure you get in close to check out the detail in its design.

Rumour has it:

The restaurant behind the sculpture cooks up a feast of crustaceans when lobsters are in season, but don't tell the Big Lobster or there's bound to be tears.

Starring role:

The philatelists (stamp boffins) at Australia Post know a great Big Thing when they see one. That's why in 2007 artist Reg Mombassa was commissioned to design a limited edition stamp featuring five of Australia's big things, including the Big Lobster.

Anything else I should know?

In 2008, a giant lobster of the edible variety, affectionately named Big Dee-Dee, became a major tourist attraction in the Canadian fishing town of Shediac, which is also home to the world's heaviest lobster statue. The crustacean was figured to be more than 100 years old and had a dominant claw as big as a size ten boot.

CHEAPEST LOBSTERS IN TOWN TODAY

Image: Wikimedia Commons, Riana Dzasta

ICONOMETRE

9/10

For being the world's tallest lobster sculpture and carrying off its pink coat without so much as a blush, we reckon Kingston's Big Lobster is one seriously iconic icon.

The Big Lobster

Introducing...
The BIG Miner

Where it's at:

Right in front of you as in come into **Kapunda** from the south side.

Vitals:

DOB: 1988

Dimensions: 7m high

The mighty miner so magnificently mounted on its mantel in Kapunda is a not-so-subtle hint that it was mining that put the town on the map. There is something sincere and moving about the statue known as Map Kernow, which means 'Son of Cornwall' in the Cornish dialect. The cheery Big Miner is a tribute to the 340 Cornish men and boys who worked the local mine during the 1800s.

Rumour has it:

Back in 1841, silver was the first mineral to be discovered in South Australia when the wheel of a cart accidentally broke off a piece of rock and exposed the precious metal.

Did you know?

From 1834 until it closed in 1878, the Kapunda mine produced more than £1 million of ore.

Starring role:

In 2006, American rock band the Foo Fighters wrote and performed a song in honour of Beaconsfield miner Brant Webb.

Anything else I should know?

There is a real sense that present-day locals are still grateful to the 340 mostly Cornish men and boys who worked the mines during the rough days of the 1800s.

Image: Pete Johns

7/10

Mining is a massive industry in Australia and played a huge role in its successful colonisation by Europeans. Without the early mines, the floundering colonies probably would have gone bankrupt.

The Big Miner

Where it's at:

Along the Old Sturt Highway just outside **Berri**, 240 km from Adelaide.

Vitals:

DOB: 1980

Dimensions: 15m tall, diameter 12m

Materials: steel and fibreglass

Introducing...

The BIG Orange

If you go down to the banks of the Murray, you're in for a Big Orange surprise. Think art gallery and cafe plus a juice bar serving you-know-what. At the top of the Big Orange, there's even a viewing platform so you see for yourself the orchards that make Berri the citrus centre of the universe.

Rumour has it:

Which came first, the colour or the fruit? Of course, it was the fruit and the colour was named in its honour. The word orange is derived from 'n ra ga' – the word for 'orange tree' in the ancient Indian language of Sanskrit. 'Orange' began fruiting in English around the 14th century.

Did you know?

The town of Berri wasn't named after a small fruit high in antioxidants, but was derived from the local Aboriginal word meaning 'a wide bend in the river.'

Starring role:

Oranges are incredibly versatile and you can do a lot more than just peel and eat them. Orange leaves can be boiled to make tea and orange peel is used by canny gardeners to repel slugs.

Anything else I should know?

While oranges have been cultivated for centuries, the tasty sweet ones only started appearing in the 15th century. Apparently, though, the ancient people aren't bitter.

Image: AAP

ICONOMETRE

6/10

It's so smooth and round and there's a whole lot happening inside. If you haven't been in and up the Big Orange, you simply haven't lived.

The Big Orange

The BIG Rocking Horse

Where it's at:

Beside the Toy Factory in **Gumeracha**, a short drive from Adelaide city centre.

Vitals:

DOB: 1984

Dimensions: 18.3m high, 17m long

Materials: steel

If you manage to drive past the Big Rocking Horse then you must immediately hand over your licence at the nearest police station. It is enormous. In fact, it's the biggest on Earth. It is also one of the best Big Things for kids as next door there's an animal park and, in case you missed it, a whopping great Toy Factory.

Rumour has it:

Rocking horses have been feeding children's dreams of becoming princesses, champion jockeys, polo players, and knights of the realm for centuries. In 2006, the Victoria and Albert Museum in London paid £25,000 for a 400 year-old rocking horse on which Charles I is rumoured to have sat.

Did you know?

If you climb to the top of the Rocking Horse you'll be awarded a certificate for your endeavour.

Starring role:

English poet and novelist D. H. Lawrence wrote a short story called 'The Rocking Horse Winner' about a boy who loved nothing more than to 'sit on his big rocking-horse, charging madly into space.'

Anything else I should know?

The town's odd name is apparently based on a misunderstanding on the part of European prospectors who misheard the local Aborigines describing a water hole along the River Torrens as 'umeracha.'

Image: Wikimedia Commons, Peripitus

The Big Rocking Horse

The BIG Scotsman

Where it's at:

Outside Scotty's Motel in the north Adelaide suburb of **Medindie**.

Vitals:

DOB: 1963

Dimensions: 5m tall

Och aye, is thar a big thing under that kilt? For many happy years, the Big Scotsman has proudly paraded with his pipes on a ledge outside Scotty's Motel. The temptation for tourists to look under his kilt must be strong, yet the Big Scotsman has managed to retain his dignity. You can hear him thinking, 'Aye, lass, thar's nothin' wrong down there. Everything is in first class workin' order.'

Rumour has it:

Scots accounted for around five per cent of convicts sent to Australia. Most of the rest were either English, Irish or Welsh, but there were also New Zealand Maoris, Chinese, Indians, and former slaves from the Caribbean.

Did you know?

Scottish men have worn the kilt since at least the 16th century. Traditionally, undergarments are not worn at the same time. The story goes that during World War I the British military enforced this rule by making soldiers stand over a mirror. Any man sporting Y-fronts would be docked his alcohol ration.

Starring role:

Aussie Mel Gibson starred in the 1995 historical epic *Braveheart* that caused a revival of Scottish nationalism, and the appearance of supporters covered in blue face paint at Scottish sporting events.

Anything else I should know?

Variations of bagpipes have been used throughout Europe and the Middle East for more than two millennia. The Scottish Great Highland Bagpipe is, however, the only musical instrument to have been banned as a weapon of war. In 1747, the English passed an Act of Parliament forbidding Scots to wear their tartan or play bagpipes in an effort to wipe out Scottish culture.

Image: Pete Johns

SCOTTY'S

The Big Scotsman

7/10

The Big Scotsman is a tribute to Scottish culture in Australia. It's an icon, Jim, but not as we know it.

The BIG Winch

Where it's at:

The outback town of **Coober Pedy**, about 846 km from Adelaide.

Vitals:

DOB: 1986, after a cyclone destroyed the original

Dimensions: about 10m tall

Materials: steel

This isn't a wind up — it's the Big Winch. Towering over the town centre, this whopper of a winch is based on the ones used to haul opals to the surface from the region's newly cut mines. With its look-out station and adjoining opal and art gallery, the Big Winch's attraction hasn't wound down yet.

Rumour has it:

Over three quarters of the town's inhabitants live underground to escape the scalding temperatures that can reach 60°C in summer. The first underground dwellers are believed to have been soldiers returning from the trenches after World War I.

Did you know?

Opal mining is at the heart of Coober Pedy's development, but it took a teenage boy named Willie Hutchinson to show the men how it's done. In 1915, he discovered the area's first opal and the town's main street is named in his honour.

Starring role:

If you feel like you've been here before then you probably have watched *Mad Max III* or *Until the End of the World* by legendary European director Wim Wenders.

Anything else I should know?

Winches are a big deal in this part of the world. Inside the world-renowned Coober Pedy Underground Catacomb Anglican Church, the altar is shaped like, you guessed right, a Big Winch.

Image: Genevieve Bell

The Big Winch

The Big Stair

The Big Crocodile

WAGIN

The Big Ram

The Big Crocodile

The Big Staircase

Western Australia

The Big Crocodile

WAGIN

The BIG Crocodile

Where it's at:

In the middle of the main street in **Wyndham**, along the Great Northern Highway, about 100 km north of Kununurra.

Vitals:

DOB:
1988

Dimensions:
20m long, 3m high

Materials:
5.5 km of steel rod, 10 rolls of bird mesh and 6 cubic metres of concrete

There are big crocs and then there's the Big Crocodile – the most gargantuan of the lot. Built by sculptor Andrew Hickson and Aboriginal students from the local TAFE, the coordinates for the ravishing reptile were computer generated from a photograph of a generously proportioned saltwater killing machine.

Rumour has it:

Nearby Cambridge Gulf is teeming with crocs that used to gather on the banks of the river, waiting for blood or leftover meat to wash down from the local meatworks. With the meatworks now closed, they're not as easy to spot but don't be fooled – they're still out there.

Did you know?

The largest recorded crocodile is a giant saltie that measured 8.6m and weighed 1,352kg weight. It was shot in Queensland in 1957.

Starring role:

For many, crocodiles have become synonymous with the work and personality of the Crocodile Hunter Steve Irwin, who dedicated his life to preserving their natural habitat.

Anything else I should know?

Surprisingly, Wyndham has a few accolades to its credit. It is the Kimberley's oldest town, Western Australia's northernmost town, and Australia's hottest town with an average maximum temperature of 35.6°C.

Image: Tammy McCoy

The Big Crocodile

The BIG Ram

Where it's at:

Two and a half hours out of Perth, in the middle of the main park at **Wagin** – Australia's sheep shearing capital of culture.

Vitals:

DOB: 14 September 1985

Dimensions: weighs 4 tonnes, 13m long, 9m high, 6m wide

Materials: fibreglass

You might find yourself going baa-listic with excitement when you catch sight of the Big Ram, or Big Baart as he's known to the locals. And it's not just people he impresses. According to legend, when the macho ram was under construction, he caught the eye of a truckload of ewes that all baaed out to get his attention.

Rumour has it:

Wagin has more sheep per capita than New Zealand.

Did you know?

The first sign of the zodiac is Aries, which originates from an ancient Greek myth about a flying ram that had a golden fleece. After rescuing a couple of spoilt rich Greek kids, the poor ram was sacrificed and its golden fleece hung on a tree and watched over by a dragon.

Starring role:

Big Baart is the centrepiece of Wagin's annual Woolorama Rural Show, an agricultural event that's second only to the Perth Royal Show. And let's face it, life for a giant ram cannot get any more showbiz than that.

Anything else I should know?

Sheep experts should be able to verify that the Big Ram is proportionally nine times the size of your average ram.

Image: Wikimedia Commons, Nachoman-au

The Big Ram

ICONOMETRE

8/10

There is a lot of local love for Big Baart. He even has the Giant Ram Tourist Park named in his honour.

The BIG Staircase

Where it's at:

A primo spot in the King's Park Botanical Gardens in **Perth**.

Vitals:

DOB: 1966 – the year England won the soccer World Cup.

Dimensions: 101 steel steps take you 15m closer to heaven.

Hey-ho, hey-ho, it's off up the spiral staircase we go. The Big Staircase is known as the DNA Tower because it looks like a double helix molecule – one of the building blocks of life. The exact DNA molecule it resembles is deoxyribonucliec acid but unless you're a rocket scientist calling it the Deoxyribonucliec Acid Tower is a bit of a mouthful.

Rumour has it:

If you run up the tower, the whole structure starts to wobble and shake. We dare you to see if it's true.

Did you know?

Even though it looks like a double helix, the original design was copied from a staircase found inside the Chateau de Blois, France.

Starring role:

Journalist Natalee Ward ranked the DNA Tower as the 8th best city lookout in Australia, which might explain why everyone who visits Perth seems to return with a picture of the view from the top.

Anything else I should know?

The DNA Tower is quite possibly the only staircase in the world designed to lead you back where you started. After climbing to the top it's a prerequisite that you take a minute to admire the vista. On a clear day you might be lucky enough to spy Rottnest Island.

Image: Ian Gallagher

8/10

When it comes to stuff that's iconic, DNA has to rank pretty high, surely.

The Big Staircase

The Big Stork

The Big Boxing Croc

The Big Stockwhip

kwhip

The Big Boxing Croc

The Big Stockwhip

The Big Boxing Croc

Northern Territory

Where it's at:

In front of the servo in **Humpty Doo**, about 47 kms from Darwin on the Arnhem Highway.

Vitals:

DOB: 1987

Dimensions: 13m tall

Materials: fibreglass

Cost: $137,000

Introducing...

The BIG Boxing Croc

You'd expect the Big Thing in a town called Humpty Doo to be a bit strange, and the Big Boxing Croc won't let you down. Not only is the reptilian hulk standing on its hind legs, but he's donned a pair of boxing gloves so raspberry red they'd make the beefiest boxing kangaroo blush.

Rumour has it:

The crocodile's reputation as fearsome predator was given a boost in 2008 when NT fisherman Paul van Bruggen photographed a saltie taking out a shark – the region's other top carnivore. The images showed a three metre croc attacking a shark in the water before dragging it onto dry land and finishing it off. And it wasn't even wearing boxing gloves.

Did you know?

The design for the Boxing Croc was inspired by the boxing kangaroo mascot used by Aussie sailors competing in the America's Cup.

Starring role:

1980s hit flick *Crocodile Dundee* introduced Paul Hogan and Aussie humour to a global audience, but how many remember that Mr Dundee earned a crust as a croc poacher?

Anything else I should know?

You really shouldn't mess with the Big Boxing Croc. He's so tough he can even withstand cyclones.

Image: Wikimedia Commons, Stuart Edwards

9/10

Does the exceptionally iconic status of a giant red-gloved, boxing crocodile really need any explanation?

The Big Boxing Croc

Where it's at:

At the entrance to Mick's Whips Homestead, 60 km south of Darwin, between **Acacia** and **Noonamah**.

Vitals:

DOB: 2003

Dimensions: 18.5m x 7.5m

Introducing...

The BIG Stockwhip

If you come across this Big Thing in the wild it can only mean one thing: you are about to learn how to crack a stockwhip. The Big Stockwhip represents the final threshold before you enter the world of whip guru Mick Denigan, who has been giving whip-cracking demonstrations for decades.

Rumour has it:

The best quality stockwhips are made from Kangaroo hide, while inferior whips are usually made with cowhide and horsehide.

Did you know?

Over the years, Mick has taught more than 30 000 people to crack a whip and has even added 'whip art' to his repertoire – the art of lashing a canvas with a paint-covered whip. These artworks would certainly make for an interesting gift or a special reminder of your trip around Australia.

Starring role:

In the early 1900s footy spectators got their half-time thrills courtesy of Mulga Fred, an Aboriginal showman who could whip a cigarette paper from the hands and lips of a brave volunteer. It's also said that he used to lie on the ground and use a stockwhip to crack paper from his own mouth.

Anything else I should know?

The Aussie stockwhip has evolved from the English hunting whip that was shipped over with the early settlers. What makes the stockwhip unique is its solid handle that can be separated from the body of the whip, so that it can be hooked over a horseman's forearm.

Image: Pete Johns

The Big Stockwhip

6/10

The sound of cracking whips is part of the air in this part of the world.

The Big Tassie Devil

The Big Penguin

The Big Penguin

The Big Tassie Devil

The Big Platypus

Tasmania

The Big Platypus

Where it's at:

Penguin, a picturesque town perched on the island's north-west coast.

Vitals:

DOB: 1975 – built to mark the centenary of the 'Proclamation of the Town of Penguin', which took place on 25 October 1875.

Dimensions: 3.15m tall

Materials: ferro-cement and fibreglass

Introducing...

The BIG Penguin

Put your flippers together for the Big Penguin – one of many models of flightless aquatic birds you will see in these parts. They really are everywhere in Penguin town, which was named by Ronald Gunn in 1861. All we can say is that he must have had quite a penchant for the local fairy penguins in whose honour he named the settlement.

Rumour has it:

The Big Penguin is a model of a fairy penguin, the smallest species of penguin. These little critters are typically around 40cm tall and weigh about one kilogram. The sculpture's design was 'borrowed' from a picture book that belonged to the daughter of the engineer commissioned to design it.

Did you know?

When it comes to size, emperor penguins are the kings, growing to an average height of just over a metre and weighing in at 30kg.

Starring role:

Penguins took over the box office by starring in the 2006 animation hit flick *Happy Feet* – a movie set in an Antarctic penguin colony where penguins sang their 'Heartsong' in order to attract their soul mate.

Anything else I should know?

Fairy penguins have to be extremely tough as they spend the whole winter at sea, returning to land for breeding in late spring and early summer. In most cases, fairy penguins have one mate for life.

Image: Wikimedia Commons, Stuart Edwards

ICONOMETRE

7/10

You either have it or you don't, and penguins have it in abundance. They can't fly, they can barely walk, but they'll always be cool. Maybe Mr Gunn was onto something.

The Big Penguin

Where it's at:

Outside the Axeman's Hall of Fame in La Trobe, 5 km south of **Devonport**.

Vitals:

DOB: 2003 and moved to its current spot in 2006

Dimensions: 8m long and 6m wide

Materials: bird wire and fibreglass

Introducing...

The BIG Platypus

This full-sized fella started life as a float in Launceston's Centenary of Federation parade. Since then, the Big Platypus has gone on to even bigger and better things. It is the town of La Trobe's top artwork and is also a beacon for 'The Platypus Experience' tourist attraction. And, if this Big one floats your fancy, you might want to check out real platypi at dusk along the banks of King's Creek.

Rumour has it:

A legend from the Aboriginal Dreamtime says the first platypus was created when a water rat mated with an unsuspecting duck that had strayed from the safety of her pond.

Did you know?

Some scientists believe that the platypus is the missing link between birds and mammal-like reptiles that lived during the Triassic Period 190 million years ago.

Starring role:

Award-winning film-makers David Parer and Liz Parer-Cook spent three years filming their epic ABC documentary *Platypus – The World's Strangest Animal*.

Anything else I should know?

They're not all cute and cuddly. Male platypi are armed with two spurs on their hind legs that can inject enough venom to kill a dog.

ICONOMETRE

9/10

Platypi and their platypups are unique to Australia's east coast. You won't find another animal remotely like them anywhere else on the planet.

The Big Platypus

Where it's at:

Out the front of the Trowunna Wildlife Park at **Mole Creek**.

Vitals:

DOB: 1980

Dimensions:
2m high, 3m long

Introducing...

The BIG Tassie Devil

They are not the prettiest peach in the pudding, but the Tassie Devil has a special place in Aussie folklore. Hunted almost to extinction after Europeans first settled at Hobart, the devils are a unique, if odd-looking part of the local landscape.

Rumour has it:

Tassie Devils love their tucker. A healthy Devil can easily eat 10 per cent of its body weight, or more, in one day.

Did you know?

Most devils look like their heads are too big for their bodies. The head and neck in older males often accounts for almost a quarter of their total weight. They evolved that way because the devils needed very powerful jaws to crunch through the bones of their prey. While they might look aggressive and dangerous, Devils are far more likely to run away than attack.

Starring role:

'Taz' the Tasmanian Devil, was a cartoon character created by Warner Bros Animation as part of its Looney Tunes cartoon series. Despite appearing in only five short animations before the company closed down in 1963, Taz went on to become a household name around the world.

Anything else I should know?

Devils, like other marsupials, have fat reserves stored in their tails, which means a devil with a big fat tail is a healthy, happy specimen.

Image: Ben Walther

ICONOMETRE

9/10

The Big Tassie Devil is a monument to all devils and especially Mickey, on whom the sculpture is modelled, and who is buried underneath it.

WUNNA
DLIFE

The Big Tassie Devil

Index

Index

The Big Banana